HISTORY'S MOST INFLUENTIAL MUSICIANS

FROM 1900 TO 1930

Charles Ives to Umm Kulthūm

EDITED BY GINI GORLINSKI

Britannica® Educational Publishing

IN ASSOCIATION WITH

ROSEN EDUCATIONAL SERVICES

Published in 2024 by Britannica Educational Publishing
(a trademark of Encyclopædia Britannica, Inc.)
in association with Rosen Educational Services, LLC
2544 Clinton Street, Buffalo, NY 14224.

Distributed exclusively by Rosen Educational Services.
For a listing of additional Britannica Educational Publishing titles, call toll free (800) 237-9932.

First Edition

Britannica Educational Publishing
Michael I. Levy: Executive Editor
Marilyn L. Barton: Senior Coordinator, Production Control
Steven Bosco: Director, Editorial Technologies
Lisa S. Braucher: Senior Producer and Data Editor
Yvette Charboneau: Senior Copy Editor
Kathy Nakamura: Manager, Media Acquisition
Gini Gorlinski, Associate Editor, Music and Dance
Diana Solomon, Copy Editor

Editor: Greg Roza
Book design: Michael Flynn

Photo credits: Cover pp. 52, 57 courtesy of the Library of Congress; p. 22 https://commons.wikimedia.org/wiki/File:Carter_Family_1927.jpg; p. 31 https://commons.wikimedia.org/wiki/File:Coleporter.jpg; https://commons.wikimedia.org/wiki/File:GershwinStandingFacingLeftBain.jpg; p. 46 https://commons.wikimedia.org/wiki/File:Duke_Ellington_1964.jpg.

Cataloging-in-Publication Data

Names: Gorlinski, Gini.
Title: Influential musicians: from 1900 to 1930 — Charles Ives to Umm Kulthūm / Gini Gorlinski.
Description: New York : Britannica Educational Publishing, in Association with Rosen Educational Services. 2024. | Series: History's most influential musicians | Includes glossary and index.
Identifiers: ISBN 9781499474978 (library bound) | ISBN 9781499474961 (pbk) | ISBN 9781499474985 (ebook)
Subjects: LCSH: Musicians--Biography--Juvenile literature. | Musicians--Juvenile literature.
Classification: LCC ML3929.G67 2024 | DDC 780.92'2 B--dc23

Manufactured in the United States of America

CPSIA Compliance Information: Batch #CSBRIT24. For further information contact Rosen Publishing at 1-800-237-9932.

CONTENTS

Introduction

"Music is my mistress, and she plays second fiddle to no one."
—Duke Ellington

What is influence? Is it the power that one individual holds to change the world? Is it prestige—the glimmering reputation earned by those who have achieved excellence or superiority? Or is it that sense of immortality bestowed on certain people who, through their lives, their actions, and their accomplishments, have climbed pedestals so high and prominent that they are virtually guaranteed a place in the books of history?

Influence can mean so many things and is therefore hard to define. But this much is clear: in a book such as this, where the subject is influential musicians, an exact definition hardly matters. Such artists may exert themselves in all kinds of ways—through their compositions, lyrics, performances, or even through "extracurricular" activities such as raising funds for charitable causes and organizations. Some musicians were inspired by influences beyond music. Visits to Paris prompted a young George Gershwin to create his famous orchestral composition *An American in Paris*.

As for the music experience and its delivery, today is quite different than just a few short years ago. Records, cassette tapes, and CDs are all but gone. In the 21st century, we have ear buds and smartphones, we stream music online from sites such as Spotify, Amazon Music, Apple Music, and Pandora. Music today is digital. It is fast, at our fingertips, and often it is free. The current profile will undoubtedly change in the future—it always does.

But then again, you can also be sure that much will be the same. We will always listen to music through whatever device we choose. Music will always be a part of our lives, ringing through our ears even when it is silent and nothing but a memory. People will always sing as they shower, turn it up as they drive, and "tune out" as they try to ignore everything else in their lives. That is music, and that is the influence it has on us.

Those musicians featured in this book span hundreds of years, countless musical genres, and immeasurable distances in style, technique, and purpose. Nevertheless, they have all been, and continue to be, influential. Some are influential because they brought a unique approach to their art that others later followed. Others were leaders of an influential movement in their field—a movement that led future musicians to improvise, change, and ultimately re-create music itself. And still others, through their work, brought about social reform and societal change that has forever shaped the landscape in which we now live.

For these influential people, music was and is life. Tchaikovsky, Stravinsky, Rachmaninoff. Springsteen, Sinatra, Madonna. They devoted their careers to the art, spending countless hours writing, creating, and fine-tuning. They have performed for great crowds, spoken on their beliefs, stood up for just causes, and above all, brought pleasure to the people who have listened. In doing so, each has left a mark, a stamp of influence, on the world.

CHARLES IVES

(b. Oct. 20, 1874, Danbury, Conn., U.S.—d. May 19, 1954, New York, N.Y.)

Charles Edward Ives was a significant American composer known for a number of innovations that anticipated most of the later musical developments of the 20th century.

Ives received his earliest musical instruction from his father, who was a bandleader, music teacher, and acoustician who experimented with the sound of quarter tones. At 12, Charles played organ in a local church, and two years later his first composition was played by the town band. In 1893 or 1894, he composed "Song for the Harvest Season," in which the four parts—for voice, trumpet, violin, and organ—were in different keys. That year he began studying at Yale University under Horatio Parker, then the foremost academic composer in the United States. His unconventionality disconcerted Parker, for whom Ives eventually turned out a series of "correct" compositions.

After graduation in 1898, Ives became an insurance clerk and part-time organist in New York City. In 1907, he founded the highly successful insurance partnership of Ives & Myrick, which he headed from 1916 to 1930. Nearly all his works were written before 1915, while operating his business, and many lay unpublished until his death. Indeed, his music became widely known only in the last years of his life. In 1947, he received the Pulitzer Prize for his *Third Symphony* (*The Camp Meeting*; composed 1904–11). His *Second Symphony* (1897–1902) was first performed in its entirety 50 years after its composition.

Ives's music is intimately related to American culture and experience, especially that of New England. His compositions—with integrated quotations from popular tunes, revival hymns, barn dances, and classical European music—are frequently works of enormous complexity that freely employ sharp dissonance, polytonal harmonies, and polymetric constructions. He drew from European music what techniques he wished while experimenting with tone clusters, microtonal intervals, and elements of chance in music. (In one bassoon part he directs the player to play whatever he wants beyond a specific point.) Believing that all sound is potential music, he was somewhat of an iconoclast.

In *The Unanswered Question* (composed before 1908), a string quartet or string orchestra repeats simple harmonies; placed apart from them, a trumpet reiterates a question-like theme that is dissonantly and confusedly commented upon by flutes (optionally with an oboe or a clarinet). In the second movement of *Three Places in New England* (also titled *First Orchestral Set* and *A New England Symphony*; 1903–14), the music gives the effect of two bands approaching and passing each other, each playing its own melody in its own key, tempo, and rhythm. His monumental *Second Piano Sonata* (subtitled *Concord, Mass., 1840–60*), which was written from 1909 to 1915 and first performed in 1938, echoes the spirit of the New England Transcendentalists in its four sections, "Emerson," "Hawthorne," "The Alcotts," and "Thoreau." It contains tone clusters, quotes Beethoven, and includes a flute obbligato honouring Thoreau's wish to hear a flute over Walden. The mood of the sonata ranges from wild and dissonant to idyllic and mystical. It was published in 1920, together with Ives's pamphlet *Essays Before a Sonata*.

Ives conceived his *Second String Quartet* (1911–13; composition on second movement begun 1907) as a conversation, political argument, and reconciliation among four men; it is full of quotations from hymns, marches, and Beethoven,

Brahms, and Tchaikovsky. His *Variations on America* (1891; additions before 1894) is the earliest polytonal piece known. In one of his piano and violin sonatas, he adds a passage for trumpet. His *114 Songs* (1919–24) for voice and piano vary from ballads to satire, hymns, protest songs, and romantic songs. In technique they range from highly complex (e.g., with tone clusters, polytonality, and atonality) to straightforward and simple.

Other compositions include *Central Park in the Dark* (1906), for chamber orchestra; *General William Booth Enters into Heaven* (1914; to Vachel Lindsay's poem), for soloist or choir and band but also performed in arrangements for chamber orchestra and for voice and piano; and the four-part symphony *A Symphony: New England Holidays* ("Washington's Birthday," 1909, rescored 1913; "Decoration Day," 1912; "Fourth of July," 1912–13; and "Thanksgiving and Forefathers' Day," 1904). The Ives manuscripts were given to the Library of the Yale School of Music by his wife, Harmony Ives, in 1955, and a temporary mimeographed catalog was compiled from 1954 to 1960 by pianist John Kirkpatrick.

BÉLA BARTÓK

(b. March 25, 1881, Nagyszentmiklós, Hung., Austria-Hungary—d. Sept. 26, 1945, New York, N.Y., U.S.)

Hungarian composer, pianist, ethnomusicologist, and teacher Béla Bartók is known for the Hungarian flavour of his major musical compositions, which include orchestral works, string quartets, piano solos, several stage works, a cantata, and a number of settings of folk songs for voice and piano.

Career in Hungary

Bartók spent his childhood and youth in various provincial towns, studying the piano with his mother and later with a succession of teachers. He began to compose small dance pieces at age nine, and two years later he played in public for the first time, including a composition of his own in his program.

Bartók undertook his professional studies in Budapest, at the Royal Hungarian Academy of Music. He developed rapidly as a pianist but less so as a composer. His discovery in 1902 of the music of Richard Strauss stimulated his enthusiasm for composition. At the same time, a spirit of optimistic nationalism was sweeping Hungary, and the 22-year-old composer wrote a symphonic poem, *Kossuth* (1903); in a style reminiscent of Strauss, though with a Hungarian flavour, the work portrays the life of the great patriot Lajos Kossuth, who had led the revolution of 1848–49. Despite a scandal at the first performance, the work was received enthusiastically.

Shortly after Bartók completed his studies in 1903, he and the Hungarian composer Zoltán Kodály, who collaborated with Bartók, discovered that what they had considered Hungarian folk music and drawn upon for their compositions was instead the music of city-dwelling Roma (Gypsies). A vast reservoir of authentic Hungarian peasant music was subsequently made known by the research of the two composers. The initial collection was begun with the intention of revitalizing Hungarian music. Both composers not only transcribed many folk tunes for the piano and other media but also incorporated into their original music elements of rural music.

Bartók was appointed to the faculty of the Academy of Music in 1907 and retained that position until 1934, when he resigned to become a working member of the Academy of Sciences. His holidays were spent collecting folk material, and he soon began the publication of articles and monographs.

At the same time, Bartók was expanding the catalog of his compositions, with many new works for the piano, a substantial number for orchestra, and the beginning of a series of six string quartets that was to constitute one of his most impressive achievements. His first numbered quartet (1908) shows few traces of folk influence, but in the others that influence is omnipresent. The quartets parallel and illuminate Bartók's stylistic development: in the second quartet (1915–17) Berber elements reflect the composer's collecting trip to North Africa; in the third (1927) and fourth (1928) there is a more intensive use of dissonance; and in the fifth (1934) and sixth (1939) there is a reaffirmation of traditional tonality.

In 1911, Bartók wrote his only opera, *Duke Bluebeard's Castle*, an allegorical treatment of the legendary wife murderer with a score permeated by characteristics of traditional Hungarian folk songs, especially in the speech-like rhythms of the text setting. The technique is comparable to that used by the French composer Claude Debussy in his opera *Pelléas et Mélisande* (1902). A ballet, *The Wooden Prince* (1914–16), and a pantomime, *The Miraculous Mandarin* (1918–19), followed; thereafter he wrote no more for the stage.

Unable to travel during World War I, Bartók devoted himself to composition and the study of the collected folk music. During the short-lived proletarian dictatorship of the Hungarian Soviet Republic in 1919, he served as a member of the Music Council with Kodály and Dohnányi. Upon its overthrow Kodály was removed from his position at the Academy of Music; but Bartók, despite his defense of his colleague, was permitted to remain.

His most productive years were the two decades that followed the end of World War I in 1918, when his musical language was completely and expressively formulated. He had assimilated many disparate influences; in addition to those already mentioned—Strauss and Debussy—there were the 19th-century Hungarian composer Franz Liszt and the modernists Igor Stravinsky and Arnold Schoenberg. Bartók arrived at a vital and varied style, rhythmically animated, in which diatonic and chromatic elements are juxtaposed without incompatibility. Within these two creative decades, Bartók composed two concerti for piano and orchestra and one for violin; the *Cantata Profana* (1930), his only large-scale choral work; the *Music for Strings, Percussion, and Celesta* (1936) and other orchestral works; and several important chamber scores, including the *Sonata for Two Pianos and Percussion* (1937). The same period saw Bartók expanding his activities as a concert pianist, playing in most of the countries of western Europe, the United States, and the Soviet Union.

U.S. Career

As Nazi Germany extended its sphere of influence in the late 1930s and Hungary appeared in imminent danger of capitulation, Bartók found it impossible to remain in his homeland. After a second concert tour of the United States in 1940, he immigrated there the same year. An appointment as research assistant in music at Columbia University, New York City, enabled him to continue working with folk music, transcribing and editing for publication a collection of Serbo-Croatian women's songs, a part of a much larger recorded collection of Yugoslav folk music. With his wife, the pianist Ditta Pásztory, he was able to give a few concerts. His health, however, had begun to deteriorate even before his arrival in the United States.

Bartók's last years were marked by the ravages of leukemia, which often prevented him from teaching, lecturing, or performing. Nonetheless, he was able to compose the *Concerto for Orchestra* (1943), the *Sonata for violin solo* (1944), and all but the last measures of the *Piano Concerto No. 3* (1945). When he died, his last composition, a viola concerto, was left an uncompleted mass of sketches (completed by Tibor Serly, 1945).

IGOR STRAVINSKY

(b. June 5 [June 17, New Style], 1882, Oranienbaum [now Lomonosov], near St. Petersburg, Russia—d. April 6, 1971, New York, N.Y., U.S.)

Russian-born composer Igor Fyodorovich Stravinsky's works had a revolutionary impact on musical thought and sensibility just before and after World War I, and his compositions remained a touchstone of modernism for much of his long career.

Early Years

Stravinsky's father was one of the leading Russian operatic basses of his day, and the mixture of the musical, theatrical, and literary spheres in the Stravinsky family household exerted a lasting influence on the composer. Nevertheless, his own musical ability emerged quite slowly. As a boy he was given lessons in piano and music theory. But then he studied law and philosophy at St. Petersburg University (graduating in 1905), and only gradually did he become aware of his aptitude for musical composition. In 1902, he showed some of his early pieces to the composer Nikolay Rimsky-Korsakov, who was sufficiently impressed to take Stravinsky as a private pupil, while at the same time advising him not to enter the conservatory for conventional academic training.

Rimsky-Korsakov tutored Stravinsky mainly in orchestration and acted as the budding composer's mentor. He also used his influence to get his pupil's music performed. Several of Stravinsky's student works were performed in the weekly gatherings of Rimsky-Korsakov's class, and two of his works for orchestra—the *Symphony in E-flat Major* and *The Faun and the Shepherdess*, a song cycle with words by Aleksandr Pushkin—were played by the Court Orchestra in 1908, the year Rimsky-Korsakov died. In February 1909, a short but brilliant orchestral piece, the *Scherzo fantastique*, was performed in St. Petersburg at a concert attended by the impresario Serge Diaghilev, who was so impressed by Stravinsky's promise as a composer that he quickly commissioned some orchestral arrangements for the summer season of his Ballets Russes in Paris. For the 1910 ballet season Diaghilev approached Stravinsky again, this time commissioning the musical score for a new full-length ballet on the subject of the Firebird.

Russian Period

The premiere of *The Firebird* at the Paris Opéra on June 25, 1910, was a dazzling success that made Stravinsky known overnight as one of the most gifted of the younger generation of composers. *The Firebird* was the first of a series of spectacular collaborations between Stravinsky and Diaghilev's company. The following year saw the Ballets Russes' premiere on June 13, 1911, of the ballet *Petrushka*, with Vaslav Nijinsky dancing the title role to Stravinsky's musical score. Meanwhile, Stravinsky had conceived the idea of writing a kind of symphonic pagan ritual to be called *Great Sacrifice*. The result was *The Rite of Spring* (*Le Sacre du printemps*), the composition of which was spread over two years (1911–13). The first performance of *The Rite of Spring* at the Théâtre des Champs Élysées on May 29,

1913, provoked one of the more famous first-night riots in the history of musical theatre. Stirred by Nijinsky's unusual and suggestive choreography and Stravinsky's creative and daring music, the audience cheered, protested, and argued among themselves during the performance, creating such a clamour that the dancers could not hear the orchestra. This highly original composition, with its shifting and audacious rhythms and its unresolved dissonances, was an early modernist landmark. From this point on, Stravinsky was known as "the composer of *The Rite of Spring*" and the destructive modernist par excellence.

Stravinsky's successes in Paris with the Ballets Russes effectively uprooted him from St. Petersburg. He had married his cousin Catherine Nossenko in 1906, and, after the premiere of *The Firebird* in 1910, he brought her and their two children to France. The outbreak of World War I in 1914 seriously disrupted the Ballets Russes' activities in western Europe, however, and Stravinsky found he could no longer rely on that company as a regular outlet for his new compositions. The war also effectively marooned him in Switzerland, where he and his family had regularly spent their winters, and it was there that they spent most of the war. The Russian Revolution of October 1917 finally extinguished any hope Stravinsky may have had of returning to his native land.

By 1914, Stravinsky was exploring a more restrained and austere, though no less vibrantly rhythmic kind of musical composition. His musical production in the following years is dominated by sets of short instrumental and vocal pieces that are based variously on Russian folk texts and idioms and on ragtime and other style models from Western popular or dance music. He expanded some of these experiments into large-scale theatre pieces. *The Wedding*, a ballet cantata begun by Stravinsky in 1914 and completed in 1923, is based on the texts of Russian village wedding songs. The "farmyard burlesque" *Renard* (1916) is similarly based on Russian folk idioms, while *The Soldier's Tale* (1918), a mixed-media piece using speech, mime, and dance accompanied by a seven-piece band, eclectically incorporates ragtime, tango, and other modern musical idioms in a series of highly infectious instrumental movements. After World War I the Russian style in Stravinsky's music began to fade, but not before it had produced another masterpiece in the *Symphonies of Wind Instruments* (1920).

Shift to Neoclassicism

The compositions of Stravinsky's first maturity—from *The Rite of Spring* in 1913 to the *Symphonies of Wind Instruments* in 1920—make use of a modal idiom based on Russian sources and are characterized by a highly sophisticated feeling for irregular metres and syncopation and by brilliant orchestral mastery. But his voluntary exile from Russia prompted him to reconsider his aesthetic stance, and the result was an important change in his music—he abandoned the Russian features of his early style and instead adopted a neoclassical idiom. Stravinsky's neoclassical works of the next 30 years usually take some point of reference in past European music—a particular composer's work or the baroque or some other historical style—as a starting point for a highly personal and unorthodox treatment that nevertheless seems to depend for its full effect on the listener's experience of the historical model from which Stravinsky borrowed.

The Stravinskys left Switzerland in 1920 and lived in France until 1939, and Stravinsky spent much of this time in Paris. (He took French citizenship in 1934.) Having lost his property in Russia during the revolution, Stravinsky was compelled to earn his living as a performer, and many of the works he composed during the 1920s and '30s were written for his own use as a concert pianist and conductor. His instrumental works of the early 1920s include the *Octet for Wind Instruments* (1923), *Concerto for Piano and Wind Instruments* (1924), *Piano Sonata* (1924), and the *Serenade in A* for piano (1925). These pieces combine a neoclassical approach to style with what seems a self-conscious severity of line and texture. Though the starkness of this approach is softened in such later instrumental pieces as the *Violin Concerto in D Major* (1931), *Concerto for Two Solo Pianos* (1932–35), and the *Concerto in E-flat* (or *Dumbarton Oaks* concerto) for 16 wind instruments (1938), a certain cool detachment persists.

Though Stravinsky was raised in the Russian Orthodox Church, his parents were not highly observant. Nonetheless, in 1926 Stravinsky experienced a reconnection to the religion of his upbringing, which in turn had a notable effect on his stage and vocal music. A religious strain can be detected in such major works as the operatic oratorio *Oedipus Rex* (1927), which uses a libretto in Latin, and the cantata *Symphony of Psalms* (1930), an overtly sacred work that is based on biblical texts. Religious feeling is also evident in the ballets *Apollon musagète* (1928) and in *Persephone* (1934). The Russian element in Stravinsky's music occasionally reemerged during this period: the ballet *The Fairy's Kiss* (1928) is based on music by Pyotr Ilyich Tchaikovsky, and the *Symphony of Psalms* has some of the antique austerity of Russian Orthodox chant, despite its Latin text.

In the years following World War I, Stravinsky's ties with Diaghilev and the Ballets Russes had been renewed, but on a much looser basis. The only new ballet Diaghilev commissioned from Stravinsky was *Pulcinella* (1920). *Apollon musagète*, Stravinsky's last ballet to be mounted by

Diaghilev, premiered in 1928, a year before Diaghilev's own death and the dissolution of his ballet company.

Later Years in the United States

In 1938, Stravinsky's oldest daughter died of tuberculosis, and the deaths of his wife and mother followed in 1939, just months before World War II broke out. Early in 1940, he married Vera de Bosset, whom he had known for many years. In autumn 1939, Stravinsky had visited the United States to deliver the Charles Eliot Norton Lectures at Harvard University (later published as the *The Poetics of Music*, 1942), and in 1940, he and his new wife settled permanently in Hollywood, California. They became U.S. citizens in 1945.

During the years of World War II, Stravinsky composed two important symphonic works, the *Symphony in C* (1938–40) and the *Symphony in Three Movements* (1942–45). The *Symphony in C* represents a summation of neoclassical principles in symphonic form, while the *Symphony in Three Movements* successfully combines the essential features of the concerto with the symphony. From 1948 to 1951 Stravinsky worked on his only full-length opera, *The Rake's Progress*, a neoclassical work (with a libretto by W. H. Auden and the American writer Chester Kallman) based on a series of moralistic engravings by the 18th-century English artist William Hogarth. *The Rake's Progress* is a mock-serious pastiche of late 18th-century grand opera but is nevertheless typically Stravinskyan in its brilliance, wit, and refinement.

The success of these late works masked a creative crisis in Stravinsky's music, and his resolution of this crisis was to produce a remarkable body of late compositions. After World War II a new musical avant-garde had emerged in Europe that rejected neoclassicism and instead claimed allegiance to the serial, or 12-tone, compositional techniques of the Viennese composers Arnold Schoenberg, Alban Berg, and especially Anton von Webern. (Serial music is based on the repetition of a series of tones in an arbitrary but fixed pattern without regard for traditional tonality.) At first this sea change threw Stravinsky into a creative depression, but he eventually emerged from it, producing a series of cautiously experimental serial works (the *Cantata*, the *Septet*, *In Memoriam Dylan Thomas*), followed by a pair of intermittently serial masterpieces, the ballet *Agon* (completed 1957) and the choral work *Canticum Sacrum* (1955). These in turn led to the choral work *Threni* (1958), a setting of the biblical Lamentations of Jeremiah in which a strict 12-tone method of composition is applied to chantlike material whose underlying character recalls that of such earlier choral works as *The Wedding* and the *Symphony of Psalms*. In his *Movements* for piano and orchestra (1959) and his orchestral *Variations* (1964), Stravinsky refined his manner still further, pursuing a variety of arcane serial techniques to support a music of increasing density and economy and possessing a brittle, diamantine brilliance. Stravinsky's serial works are generally much briefer than his tonal works but have a denser musical content.

Though always in mediocre health, Stravinsky continued full-scale creative work until 1966. His last major work, *Requiem Canticles* (1966), is a profoundly moving adaptation of modern serial techniques to a personal imaginative vision that was deeply rooted in his Russian past. This piece is an amazing tribute to the creative vitality of a composer then in his middle 80s.

LEADBELLY

(b. Jan. 21, 1885?, Jeter Plantation, near Mooringsport, La., U.S.—d. Dec. 6, 1949, New York, N.Y.)

In conjunction with his notoriously violent life, the ability of American folk-blues singer, songwriter, and guitarist Huddie William Ledbetter—better known as Leadbelly—to perform a vast repertoire of songs made him a legend.

Musical from childhood, Leadbelly played accordion, 6- and 12-string guitar, bass, and harmonica. He led a wandering life, learning songs by absorbing oral tradition. For a time he worked as an itinerant musician with Blind Lemon Jefferson. In 1918, he was imprisoned in Texas for murder. According to legend, he won his early release in 1925 by singing a song for the governor of Texas when he visited the prison. "Please Pardon Me," written and performed by a repentant Leadbelly, undoubtedly helped, but good behaviour throughout his sentence was certainly a factor as well.

Resuming a life of drifting, Leadbelly was imprisoned for attempted murder in 1930 in the Angola, La., prison farm. There he was "discovered" by the folklorists John Lomax and Alan Lomax, who were collecting songs for the Library of Congress. A campaign spearheaded by the Lomaxes secured his release in 1934, and he embarked on a concert tour of eastern colleges. Subsequently he published 48 songs and commentary (1936) about Depression-era conditions of Blacks and recorded extensively. His first commercial recordings were made for the American Record Corporation, which did not take advantage of his huge folk repertory but rather encouraged him to sing blues. He settled in New York City in 1937, struggled to make enough money, and in 1939–40 he was jailed again, this time for assault. When he was released, he worked with Woody Guthrie, Sonny Terry, Brownie McGhee, and others as the Headline Singers, performed on radio, and, in 1945, appeared in a short film. In 1949, shortly before his death, he gave a concert in Paris.

Leadbelly died penniless, but within six months his song "Goodnight, Irene" had become a million-record hit for the singing group the Weavers; along with other pieces from his repertoire, among them "The Midnight Special" and "Rock Island Line," "Goodnight, Irene" became a standard.

Leadbelly's legacy is extraordinary. His recordings reveal his mastery of a great variety of song styles and his prodigious memory; his repertory included more than 500 songs. His rhythmic guitar playing and unique vocal accentuations make his body of work both instructive and compelling. Leadbelly's influence on later musicians—including Eric Clapton, Bob Dylan, Janis Joplin, and Kurt Cobain—was immense.

CARTER FAMILY

The group consisted of Alvin Pleasant Carter, known as A.P. Carter (b. April 15, 1891, Maces Spring, Va., U.S.—d. Nov. 7, 1960, Kentucky), his wife, Sara, née Sara Dougherty (b. July 21, 1898, Flatwoods, Va., U.S.—d. Jan. 8, 1979, Lodi, Calif.), and his sister-in-law Maybelle Carter, née Maybelle Addington (b. May 10, 1909, Nickelsville, Va., U.S.—d. Oct. 23, 1978, Nashville, Tenn.).

The Carter Family was a singing group that was a leading force in the spread and popularization of the songs of the Appalachian Mountain region of the eastern United States.

The family's recording career began in 1927 in response to an advertisement placed in a local newspaper by a talent scout for Victor Records. Over the next 16 years, with two of Sara's children and three of Maybelle's (Helen, June, and Anita) also appearing, they recorded more than 300 songs for various labels, covering a significant cross section of the mountain music repertory, including old ballads and humorous songs, sentimental pieces from the 19th and early 20th centuries, and many religious pieces. They later performed extensively on radio, popularizing many songs that became standards of folk and country music, including "Jimmy Brown, the Newsboy," "Wabash Cannonball," "It Takes a Worried Man to Sing a Worried Song," and "Wildwood Flower."

The Carter Family was remarkable not only for its prolific recording but also for the musical accomplishment—and balance—of its members. A.P. was the group's songsmith. He was an avid collector of oral tradition, as well as an adept arranger of rural regional repertoire for consumption by a broader audience. A.P. also composed many new songs for the group, replicating the style of the traditional material. Sara, with her strong soprano voice, was typically the lead singer, supported by Maybelle's alto harmonies and A.P.'s bass and baritone interjections. The instrumental anchor of the Carter Family was Maybelle, a skilled performer on guitar, banjo, and autoharp. She also developed a unique finger-picking technique on guitar that continues to be emulated by many guitarists today.

In 1943, the Carter Family disbanded, its members subsequently forming various other groups. Maybelle ("Mother") Carter performed both with her daughters and as a soloist. In the 1950s, the Carter Family re-formed and appeared intermittently, with a changing lineup. The original Carter Family was the first group admitted to the Country Music Hall of Fame.

Maybelle also sang periodically with her son-in-law Johnny Cash, whose gritty songs of social commentary had already propelled him to the top of the country-and-western music industry. Known for his black clothes and

This photograph of A.P., Maybelle, and Sara Carter was taken in 1927.

rebellious persona, Cash married June Carter in 1968 during a period of waning popularity, after she helped him combat his drug addiction. The signal event in Cash's turnaround was the album *Johnny Cash at Folsom Prison* (1968), recorded live at California's Folsom Prison. He won a new generation of fans in 1994 after the release of his acoustic album *American Recordings*. The recipient of numerous awards, Cash won 13 Grammy Awards, including a lifetime achievement award in 1999, and 9 Country Music Association Awards. Cash was elected to the Country Music Hall of Fame in 1980 and to the Rock and Roll Hall of Fame in 1992. In 1996 he received a Kennedy Center Honor.

SERGEY PROKOFIEV

(b. April 23 [April 11, Old Style], 1891, Sontsovka, Ukraine, Russian Empire—d. March 5, 1953, Moscow, Russia, U.S.S.R.)

Twentieth-century Russian (and Soviet) composer Sergey Sergeyevich Prokofiev wrote in a wide range of musical genres, including symphonies, concerti, film music, operas, ballets, and program pieces.

Prerevolutionary Period

Prokofiev was born into a family of agriculturalists. Village life, with its peasant songs, left a permanent imprint on him. His mother, a good pianist, became the child's first mentor in music and arranged trips to the opera in Moscow. Meanwhile, the Russian composer Reinhold Glière twice went to Sontsovka in the summer months to train and prepare young Sergey for entrance into the conservatory at St. Petersburg. Prokofiev's years at the conservatory—1904 to 1914—were a period of swift creative growth, and when he graduated he was awarded the Anton

Rubinstein Prize in piano for a brilliant performance of his own first large-scale work—the *Piano Concerto No. 1 in D-flat Major*.

Contacts with the then new currents in theatre, poetry, and painting played an important role in Prokofiev's development. He was attracted by the work of modernist Russian poets; by the paintings of the Russian followers of Paul Cézanne and Pablo Picasso; and by the theatrical ideas of Vsevolod Meyerhold. In 1914, Prokofiev became acquainted with the ballet impresario Serge Diaghilev, who became one of his most influential advisers for the next decade and a half.

The prerevolutionary period of Prokofiev's work was marked by intense exploration. The harmonic thought and design of his work grew more and more complicated. Prokofiev wrote the ballet *Ala and Lolli* (1914), on themes of ancient Slav mythology, for Diaghilev, who rejected it. Thereupon, Prokofiev reworked the music into the *Scythian Suite* for orchestra. Its premiere, in 1916, caused a scandal but was the culmination of his career in Petrograd (St. Petersburg). The ballet *The Tale of the Buffoon Who Outjested Seven Buffoons* (1915; reworked as *The Buffoon*, 1915–20), also commissioned by Diaghilev, was based on a folktale; it served as a stimulus for Prokofiev's searching experiments in the renewal of Russian music. Prokofiev also was active in the field of opera. In 1915–16, he composed *The Gambler*, a brilliant adaptation of the novella by Fyodor Dostoyevsky. Continuing the operatic tradition of Modest Mussorgsky, Prokofiev skillfully combined subtle lyricism, satiric malice, narrative precision, and dramatic impact. During this period, Prokofiev achieved great recognition for his first two piano concerti—the first the one-movement *Concerto in D-flat Major* (1911) and the second the dramatic four-movement *Concerto in G Minor* (1913).

The year 1917—during which there were two Russian revolutions—was astonishingly productive for Prokofiev. As if inspired by feelings of social and national renewal, he wrote within one year an immense quantity of new music: he composed two sonatas, the *Violin Concerto No. 1 in D Major*, the *Classical Symphony*, and the choral work *Seven, They Are Seven*; he began the magnificent *Piano Concerto No. 3 in C Major*; and he planned a new opera, *The Love for Three Oranges*, after a comedy tale by the 18th-century Italian dramatist Carlo Gozzi, as translated and adapted by Meyerhold. In the summer of 1917, Prokofiev was included in the Council of Workers in the Arts, which led Russia's left wing of artistic activity. He later concluded that music had no place in the council's activities and decided to leave Russia temporarily to undertake a concert tour abroad.

Foreign Period

The next decade and a half are commonly called the foreign period of Prokofiev's work. For a number of reasons, chiefly the continued blockade of the Soviet Union, he could not return at once to his homeland. The first five years of Prokofiev's life abroad are usually characterized as the "years of wandering." In the summer of 1918, he gave several concerts in Japan, and in the United States his piano recitals in New York City evoked both delight and denunciation. In Chicago he was given a commission for a comic opera; *The Love for Three Oranges* was completed in 1919, though it was not produced until 1921.

In America, Prokofiev met a young singer of Spanish descent. Born Carlina Codina in Madrid and raised in New York, Lina Llubera eventually became his wife and the mother of two of his sons, Svyatoslav and Oleg. Not finding continuing support in the United States, the composer set out in the spring of 1920 for Paris for meetings with Diaghilev and the conductor Serge Koussevitzky. They soon secured for him wide recognition in the most important western European musical centres. The production of *The Buffoon* by Diaghilev's ballet troupe in Paris and London in 1921 and the Paris premiere of the *Scythian Suite* in 1921 and that of *Seven, They Are Seven* in 1924 consolidated his reputation as a brilliant innovator. The successful performance of his *Piano Concerto No. 3* (1921) also marked one of the peaks of Prokofiev's dynamic national style.

During 1922–23, Prokofiev spent more than a year and a half in southern Germany, in the Bavarian town of Ettal. There he prepared many of his compositions for the printer and also continued work on the opera *The Flaming Angel*, after a story by the contemporary Russian author Valery Bryusov. The opera, which required many years of work (1919–27), did not find a producer within Prokofiev's lifetime.

In the autumn of 1923, Prokofiev settled in Paris, where he was in close touch with progressive French musical figures, such as the composers Francis Poulenc and Arthur Honegger. Vexed by criticisms of his melodically lucid *Violin Concerto No. 1*, which had its premiere in Paris in 1923, he addressed himself to a search for a more avant-garde style. These tendencies appeared in several compositions of the early 1920s, including the epic *Symphony No. 2 in D Minor* and the *Symphony No. 3 in C Minor* (1928). In close collaboration with Diaghilev, Prokofiev created new one-act ballets, *Le Pas d'acier* (performed in 1927) and *The Prodigal Son* (performed in 1929). *Le Pas d'acier* had a sensational success in Paris and London, with its bold evocation of images of Soviet Russia at the beginning of the 1920s. *The Prodigal Son* had a lofty biblical theme and music that was exquisitely lyrical. It reflects an emotional relaxation and a clarification of style that are also seen in the *String Quartet*

No. 1 in B Minor (1930), in the *Sonata for Two Violins in C Major* (1932), and in the ballet *On the Dnieper* (1932).

In 1927, Prokofiev toured the Soviet Union and was rapturously received by the Soviet public as a world-renowned Russian musician-revolutionary. During the 1920s and the early '30s, Prokofiev also toured with immense success as a pianist in the great musical centres of western Europe and the United States. His U.S. tours were attended with tumultuous success and brought him new commissions, such as the *Symphony No. 4 in C Major* (1930), for the 50th anniversary of the Boston Symphony, and the *String Quartet No. 1*, commissioned by the Library of Congress. His new piano concerti—*No. 4* (1931), for the left hand, and *No. 5 in G Major* (1932)—demonstrated anew his bent for virtuoso brilliance.

Soviet Period

Although he enjoyed many aspects of life in the West, Prokofiev increasingly missed his homeland. Visits to the Soviet Union in 1927, 1929, and 1932 led him to return to Moscow permanently. From 1933 to 1935 the composer became a leading figure of Soviet culture. In the two decades constituting the Soviet period of Prokofiev's work—1933 to 1953—the realistic and epic traits of his art became more clearly defined. The synthesis of traditional tonal and melodic means with the stylistic innovations of 20th-century music was more fully realized.

In the years preceding World War II, Prokofiev created a number of classical masterpieces, including his *Violin Concerto No. 2 in G Minor* (1935) and the ballet *Romeo and Juliet* (1935–36). His work in theatre and the cinema gave rise to a number of programmatic suites, such as the *Lieutenant Kije* suite (1934), the *Egyptian Nights* suite (1934), and the symphonic children's tale *Peter and the Wolf* (1936).

Turning to opera, he cast in the form of a contemporary drama of folk life his *Semyon Kotko*, depicting events of the civil war in the Ukraine (1939). The basis of the opéra bouffe *Betrothal in a Monastery* (composed in 1940, produced in 1946) was the play *The Duenna*, by the 18th-century British dramatist Richard Brinsley Sheridan. Testing his powers in other genres, he composed the monumental *Cantata for the 20th Anniversary of the October Revolution* (1937), on texts by Karl Marx, V. I. Lenin, and Joseph Stalin, and the cantata *The Toast* (1939), composed for Stalin's 60th birthday.

On his last trip abroad, in 1938, Prokofiev visited Hollywood, where he studied the technical problems of the sound film; he applied what he learned to the music for Sergey Eisenstein's film *Alexander Nevsky*, depicting the 13th-century heroic Russian struggle against the Teutonic Knights. The cantata *Alexander Nevsky* was based on the music of the film.

On the eve of World War II, he left his wife and sons for poet Mira Mendelssohn, who became his second (common-law) wife. Regardless of the difficulties of the war years, he composed with remarkable assiduity, even when the evacuation of Moscow in 1941 prevented him from returning to the city until 1944. From the first days of the war, his attention was centred on a very large-scale operatic project: an opera based on Leo Tolstoy's novel *War and Peace*. He was fascinated by the parallels between 1812, when Russia crushed Napoleon's invasion, and the then-current situation. Those who heard the work were struck both by its immensity of scale (13 scenes, more than 60 characters) and by its unique blend of epic narrative with lyrical scenes depicting the personal destinies of the major characters. His increasing predilection for national-epical imagery is manifested in the heroic majesty of the *Symphony No. 5 in B-flat Major* (1944) and in the music (composed 1942–45) for Eisenstein's two-part film *Ivan the*

Terrible (Part I, 1944; Part II, 1948). Living in the Caucasus, in Central Asia, and in the Urals, the composer was everywhere interested in folklore, an interest that was reflected in the *String Quartet No. 2 in F Major* (1941), and in the projected comic opera *Khan Buzai* (never completed), on themes of Kazakh folktales.

Overwork was fatal to the composer's health, as was the stress he suffered in 1948, when he was censured by the Central Committee of the Soviet Communist Party for "formalism." During the last years of his life, Prokofiev seldom left his villa in a suburb of Moscow. His propensity for innovation, however, is still evident in such works as the *Symphony No. 6 in E-flat Minor* (1945–47), which is laden with reminiscence of the tragedies of the war just past; the *Sinfonia Concerto for Cello and Orchestra in E Minor* (1950–52), composed with consultation from the conductor and cellist Mstislav Rostropovich; and the *Violin Sonata in F Minor* (1938–46), dedicated to the violinist David Oistrakh, which is laden with Russian folk imagery. Just as in earlier years, the composer devoted the greatest part of his energy to musical theatre, as in the opera *The Story of a Real Man* (1947–48), the ballet *The Stone Flower* (1948–50), and the oratorio *On Guard for Peace* (1950). The lyrical *Symphony No. 7 in C-sharp Minor* (1951–52) was the composer's swan song.

In 1953 Prokofiev died suddenly of cerebral hemorrhage. On his worktable there remained a pile of unfinished compositions. The subsequent years saw a rapid growth of his popularity in the Soviet Union and abroad. In 1957 he was posthumously awarded the Soviet Union's highest honour, the Lenin Prize, for his *Symphony No. 7*.

COLE PORTER

(b. June 9, 1891, Peru, Ind., U.S.—d. Oct. 15, 1964, Santa Monica, Calif.)

American composer and lyricist Cole Albert Porter brought a worldly élan to the American musical, embodying in his life the sophistication of his songs.

Porter was the grandson of a millionaire speculator, and the moderately affluent circumstances of his life probably contributed to the poise and urbanity of his musical style. He began violin study at the age of 6 and piano at 8; he composed an operetta in the style of Gilbert and Sullivan at 10 and saw his first composition, a waltz, published a year later. As a student at Yale University (B.A., 1913), he composed about 300 songs, including "Eli," "Bulldog," and "Bingo Eli Yale," and wrote college shows; later he studied at Harvard Law School (1914) and Harvard Graduate School of Arts and Sciences in music (1915–16). He made his Broadway debut with the musical comedy *See America First* (1916), which, however, closed after 15 performances.

In 1917, after the United States had entered World War I, Porter went to France. (He was not, as later reported, in French military service.) He became an itinerant playboy in Europe and, though rather openly homosexual, married a wealthy, older American divorcée, Linda Lee Thomas, on Dec. 18, 1919; they spent the next two decades in lively partying and social traveling, sometimes together, sometimes apart.

In 1928, Porter composed several songs for the Broadway success *Paris*, which led to a string of hit musical comedies, including *Fifty Million Frenchmen* (1929), *Gay Divorcée* (1932), *Anything Goes* (1934), *Red, Hot and Blue* (1934), *Jubilee* (1935), *Dubarry Was a Lady* (1939), *Panama Hattie* (1940), *Kiss Me, Kate* (1948, based on William Shakespeare's *The Taming of the Shrew*), *Can-Can* (1953), and

Porter's most popular musical is Kiss Me, Kate. *This musical won the Tony Award for Best Musical in 1949. Porter won the Tony Award for Best Original Score that same year.*

Silk Stockings (1955). He concurrently worked on a number of motion pictures. Over the years he wrote such glittering songs and lyrics as "Night and Day," "I Get a Kick Out of You," "Begin the Beguine," "I've Got You Under My Skin," "In the Still of the Night," "Just One of Those Things," "Love for Sale," "My Heart Belongs to Daddy," "Too Darn Hot," "It's Delovely," "I Concentrate on You," "Always True to You in My Fashion," and "I Love Paris." He was especially adept at the catalog song, his best-known efforts being "Let's Do It" and "You're the Top."

Porter was one of the wittiest of all lyricists, with a subtlety of expression and a mastery of the interior rhyme. His work continues to stand as the epitome of sophisticated, civilized detachment in the popular song form. His large output might have been even more vast had not a horse-riding accident in 1937 left him a semi-invalid, necessitating 30 operations and the eventual amputation of a leg.

JIMMIE RODGERS

(b. Sept. 8, 1897, Pine Springs Community, near Meridian, Miss., U.S.—d. May 26, 1933, New York City, N.Y.)

American singer, songwriter, and guitarist Jimmie Rodgers (byname of James Charles Rodgers) was one of the principal figures in the emergence of the country and western style of popular music.

Rodgers, whose mother died when he was a young boy, was the son of an itinerant railroad gang foreman, and his youth was spent in a variety of southern towns and cities. Having already run away with a medicine show by age 13, he left school for good at age 14. Rodgers began working on his father's railroad crews, initially as a water carrier, and during this time was likely exposed to the work songs and early blues of African American labourers. As a young man he held a number of jobs with the railroad, including those of baggage master, flagman, and brakeman, crisscrossing the Southwest but especially working the line between New Orleans and Meridian, Miss. Early on, Rodgers aspired to be an entertainer. He learned to play the guitar and banjo, honing what became his characteristic sound—a blend of traditional country, work, blues, hobo, and cowboy songs—that ultimately earned him the nickname the "Singing Brakeman."

After contracting tuberculosis, Rodgers was forced to give up railroad work in 1924 or 1925 and began pursuing a performing career, playing everything from tent shows to street corners but with little success. He relocated to Asheville, N.C., and began appearing on local radio in 1927, backed by a string band. Following a disagreement with the band, Rodgers recorded as a guitar-playing solo artist. The popularity of his first recording, "Sleep, Baby, Sleep," sparked a long series of hits from among more than 110 recordings he would make in what proved to be a relatively short career (1928–33) that coincided with the beginning of the Great Depression. Rodgers toured widely in the South (also playing the vaudeville circuit) and, seeking a dry climate for his health, eventually settled in Texas.

Rodgers helped establish the template for country music and the model for country singers, infusing his performances and compositions with personality, humour, and heightened emotion, delivered in a unique vocal style at a time when "hillbilly music" consisted largely of old-time instrumentalists and singers who sounded much the same. Rodgers is perhaps best remembered for his distinctive blue yodel; it was popularized in "Blue Yodel No. 1" and was at the heart of some dozen other recorded versions. He was affectionately called "America's Blue Yodeler" by many of his fans. Most of Rodgers's original compositions were written with a variety of collaborators, the most prominent of whom was his sister-in-law, Elsie

McWilliams. His hits, which span the emotional gauntlet and incorporate elements of a wide variety of genres, include "Miss the Mississippi and You," "Daddy and Home," "Waiting for a Train," "Brakeman's Blues," and "Mississippi River Blues," among others. Rodgers recorded right up to his premature death, resting on a cot in the studio between takes during recording sessions. He was the first person inducted into the Country Music Hall of Fame.

FLETCHER HENDERSON

(b. Dec. 18, 1897, Cuthbert, Ga., U.S.—d. Dec. 29, 1952, New York, N.Y.)

Fletcher Hamilton Henderson, Jr., (born James Fletcher Henderson) was an American musical arranger, bandleader, and pianist who was a leading pioneer in the sound, style, and instrumentation of big band jazz.

Henderson was born into a middle-class family; his father was a school principal and his mother a teacher. He changed his name (James was his grandfather's name, Fletcher Hamilton his father's) in 1916 when he entered Atlanta University, from which he graduated as a chemistry and math major. In 1920, he moved to New York, intending to work as a chemist while pursuing a graduate degree. Although he found a part-time laboratory job, he immediately began getting work as a pianist. Within months he was a full-time musician, and he began working for W. C. Handy's music publishing company as a song plugger (i.e., promoting songs to performers). In 1921, he took a position as musical factotum for Black Swan records, the first black-owned recording company, for which he organized small bands to provide backing for such singers as Ethel Waters. He played piano for leading Black singers on more than 150 records between 1921 and 1923 and then began a full-time career as a bandleader.

Although Henderson had shown an interest in music

from childhood, when his mother taught him piano, he knew little about jazz until he was in his 20s. His orchestra, made up of well-established New York musicians, at first played standard dance-band fare, with occasional ragtime and jazz inflections. The band became more jazz-oriented in 1924 when Henderson hired the young trumpeter Louis Armstrong. At about the same time, the band's musical director and alto saxophonist, Don Redman, conceived the arrangements and instrumentation that would become the standard for big bands. The rhythm section was established as piano, bass, guitar, and drums; and the trumpet, trombone, and reed sections composed the front line. Arrangements were constructed in the call-and-response manner (e.g., the brass section "calls," the reed section "responds"), and many tunes were based upon "riffs," identifiable musical passages repeated throughout the song.

Henderson was a superb arranger but a poor businessman. Although the band had played major venues and been heard on the radio and in recordings, the band's finances were frequently in disarray, and musicians often left without notice to join other bands. He nevertheless managed to keep his band going until the mid-1930s, at which time he sold many of his arrangements to Benny Goodman, who used them to define the sound of his new band. "King Porter Stomp," "Down South Camp Meetin'," "Bugle Call Rag," "Sometimes I'm Happy," and "Wrappin' It Up" are among the Henderson arrangements that became Goodman hits.

Through the Goodman band, Henderson's arrangements became a blueprint for the sound of the swing era. Henderson arranged for Goodman for several years and formed a short-lived band of his own in 1936. That year, Henderson issued "Christopher Columbus," which became the biggest hit released under his own name. Henderson had little success in his subsequent attempts to organize bands and spent most of the 1940s arranging for Goodman, Count Basie, and others. He formed a sextet in 1950 that became the house band at New York's Cafe Society, but he suffered a stroke soon thereafter and was forced to retire.

BESSIE SMITH

(b. April 15, 1898?, Chattanooga, Tenn., U.S.—d. Sept. 26, 1937, Clarksdale, Miss.)

American singer Bessie Smith was one of the greatest of blues vocalists.

Smith grew up in poverty and obscurity. She may have made a first public appearance at the age of eight or nine at the Ivory Theatre in her hometown. About 1919, she was discovered by Gertrude "Ma" Rainey, one of the first of the great blues singers, from whom she received some training. For several years Smith traveled through the South singing in tent shows and bars and theatres in small towns. After 1920, she made her home in Philadelphia, and it was there that she was first heard by a representative of Columbia Records. In February 1923, she made her first recordings, including the classic "Down Hearted Blues," which became an enormous success, selling more than 2 million copies. She made 160 recordings in all, in many of which she was accompanied by some of the great jazz musicians of the time, including Fletcher Henderson, Benny Goodman, and Louis Armstrong.

Bessie Smith's subject matter was the classic material of the blues: poverty and oppression, love—betrayed or unrequited—and stoic acceptance of defeat at the hands of a cruel and indifferent world. The great tragedy of her career was that she outlived the topicality of her idiom. In the late 1920s, her record sales and her fame diminished as social forces changed the face of popular music and bowdlerized the earthy realism of the sentiments she expressed in her music. Her gradually increasing alcoholism caused managements to become wary of engaging her.

Known in her lifetime as the "Empress of the Blues," Smith was a bold, confident artist who often disdained the use of a microphone. Her art expressed the frustrations and hopes of a whole generation of Black Americans. She died from injuries sustained in a road accident.

GEORGE GERSHWIN

(b. Sept. 26, 1898, Brooklyn, N.Y., U.S.—d. July 11, 1937, Hollywood, Calif.)

George Gershwin, born Jacob Gershvin, was one of the most significant and popular American composers of all time. He wrote primarily for the Broadway musical theatre, but important as well are his orchestral and piano compositions in which he blended, in varying degrees, the techniques and forms of classical music with the stylistic nuances and techniques of popular music and jazz.

Early Career and Influences

Gershwin was the son of Russian-Jewish immigrants. Although his family and friends were not musically inclined, Gershwin developed an early interest in music through his exposure to the popular and classical compositions he heard at school and in penny arcades. He began his musical education at age 11, when his family bought a second-hand upright piano, ostensibly so that George's older sibling, Ira, could learn the instrument. When George surprised everyone with his fluid playing of a popular song, which he had taught himself by following the keys on a neighbour's player piano, his parents decided that George would be the family member to receive lessons.

Gershwin continued to broaden his musical knowledge and compositional technique throughout his career with various mentors. After dropping out of school at age 15, he earned an income by making piano rolls for player pianos and by playing in New York nightclubs. His most important job in this period was his stint as a song plugger, working very long hours demonstrating sheet music for the Jerome Remick music-publishing company. Although Gershwin's burgeoning creativity was hampered by his three-year stint in "plugger's purgatory," it was nevertheless an experience that greatly improved his dexterity and increased his skills at improvisation and transposing. While still in his teens, Gershwin worked as an accompanist for popular singers and as a rehearsal pianist for Broadway musicals. In 1916, he composed his first published song, "When You Want 'Em You Can't Get 'Em (When You've Got 'Em You Don't Want 'Em)," as well as his first solo piano composition, "Rialto Ripples." He began to attract the attention of Broadway luminaries.

These early experiences greatly increased Gershwin's knowledge of jazz and popular music. He enjoyed especially the songs of Irving Berlin and Jerome Kern and he was inspired by their work to compose for the Broadway stage. In 1919, entertainer Al Jolson performed the Gershwin song "Swanee" in the musical *Sinbad*; it became an enormous success, selling more than 2 million recordings and a million copies of sheet music, and making Gershwin an overnight celebrity. Also in 1919, Gershwin composed his first "serious" work, the *Lullaby* for string quartet.

Rhapsody in Blue

During the next few years, Gershwin contributed songs to various Broadway shows and revues. From 1920 to 1924, he

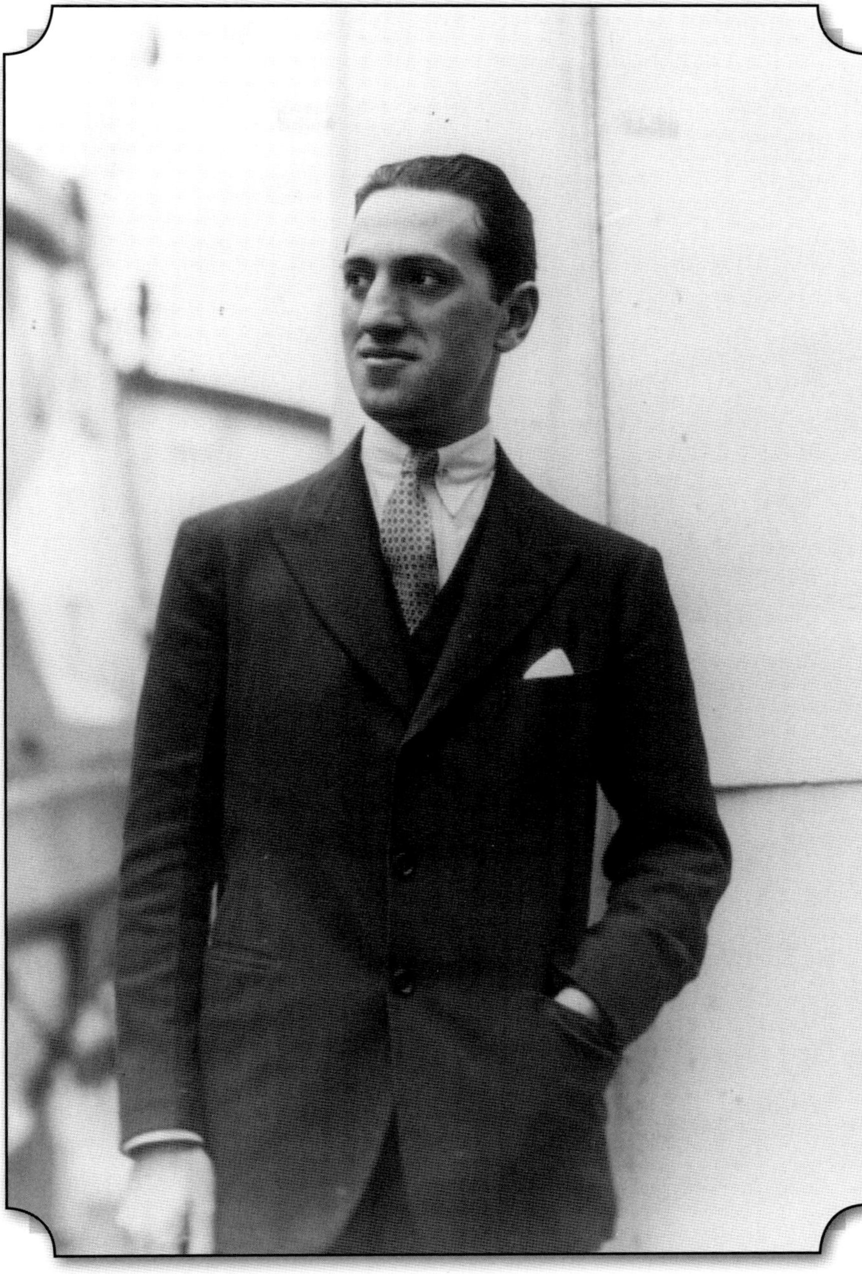

Gershwin began working for Tin Pan Alley—a group of music publishers and musicians in New York City—when he was just 15 years old.

composed scores for the annual productions of George White's *Scandals*, the popular variety revue. For the *Scandals* production of 1922, Gershwin convinced producer White to incorporate a one-act jazz opera. This work, *Blue Monday,* was poorly received and was removed from the show after one performance. Bandleader Paul Whiteman, who had conducted the pit orchestra for the show, was nevertheless impressed by the piece. He and Gershwin shared the common goal of bringing respectability to jazz music. To this end, in late 1923, Whiteman asked Gershwin to compose a piece for an upcoming concert. Legend has it that Gershwin forgot about the request until early January 1924, when he read a newspaper article announcing that the Whiteman concert on February 12 would feature a major new Gershwin composition. Writing at a furious pace in order to meet the deadline, Gershwin composed *Rhapsody in Blue*, perhaps his best-known work, in three weeks' time.

Owing to the haste in which it was written, *Rhapsody in Blue* was somewhat unfinished at its premiere. Gershwin improvised much of the piano solo during the performance, and conductor Whiteman had to rely on a nod from Gershwin to cue the orchestra at the end of the solo. Nevertheless, the piece was a resounding success and brought Gershwin worldwide fame. The revolutionary work incorporated trademarks of the jazz idiom (blue notes, syncopated rhythms, onomatopoeic instrumental effects) into a symphonic context. Arranged by Ferde Grofé (composer of the *Grand Canyon Suite*) for either symphony orchestra or jazz band, the work is perhaps the most-performed and most-recorded orchestral composition of the 20th century.

Popular Songs

For the remainder of his career, Gershwin devoted himself to both popular songs and orchestral compositions. His Broadway shows from the 1920s and '30s featured numerous songs that became standards, including: "Fascinating Rhythm," "Oh, Lady Be Good," "Sweet and Low-Down," "Someone to Watch over Me," "Strike Up the Band," "The Man I Love," "'S Wonderful," "Embraceable You," and "But Not for Me." He also composed several songs for Hollywood films, such as "Let's Call the Whole Thing Off," "They All Laughed," "A Foggy Day," "Nice Work If You Can Get It," and "Love Walked In." His lyricist for nearly all of these tunes was his older brother, Ira, whose glib, witty lyrics—often punctuated with slang, puns, and wordplay—received nearly as much acclaim as George's compositions. The Gershwin brothers comprised a somewhat unique songwriting partnership in that George's melodies usually came first—a reverse of the process employed by most composing teams.

One of the Gershwins' best-known collaborations, "I Got Rhythm," was introduced by Ethel Merman in the musical *Girl Crazy* (1930). The following year, Gershwin scored a lengthy, elaborate piano arrangement of the song, and in late 1933 he arranged the piece into a set of variations for piano and orchestra; *"I Got Rhythm" Variations* has since become one of Gershwin's most-performed orchestral works. Gershwin's piano score for "I Got Rhythm" was part of a larger project begun in 1931, *George Gershwin's Songbook*, a collection of Gershwin's personal favourite hit tunes, adapted "for the above-average pianist."

Other Works for Orchestra

In 1925, Gershwin was commissioned by the Symphony

Society of New York to write a concerto. The resulting work, *Concerto in F* (1925), Gershwin's lengthiest composition, was divided into three traditional concerto movements. The first movement loosely follows a sonata structure of exposition, development, and recapitulation. The second movement is a slow, meditative adaptation of blues progressions, and the third movement introduces new themes and returns, rondo-like, to the themes of the first. Although not as well received at the time as *Rhapsody in Blue*, the *Concerto in F* eventually came to be regarded as one of Gershwin's most important works.

An American in Paris (1928), Gershwin's second-most famous orchestral composition, was inspired by the composer's trips to Paris throughout the 1920s. His stated intention with the work was to "portray the impressions of an American visitor in Paris as he strolls about the city, listens to various street noises, and absorbs the French atmosphere." It is this piece that perhaps best represents Gershwin's employment of both jazz and classical forms. The harmonic structure of *An American in Paris* is rooted in blues traditions, and soloists are often required to bend, slide, and growl certain notes and passages, in the style of jazz musicians of the 1920s.

Gershwin's other major orchestral compositions have grown in stature and popularity throughout the years. His *Second Rhapsody* (1931) was featured, in embryonic form, as incidental music in the film *Delicious* (1931). Gershwin's *Cuban Overture* (1932), employed rhumba rhythms and such percussion instruments as claves, maracas, bongo drums, and gourds, all of which were generally unknown at the time in the United States.

Porgy and Bess

Throughout his career, Gershwin had major successes

on Broadway with shows such as *Lady, Be Good!* (1924), *Strike Up the Band* (1930), and, especially, the political satire *Of Thee I Sing* (1931), for which Ira and librettists George S. Kaufman and Morrie Ryskind shared a Pulitzer Prize. These shows, smash hits in their time, are (save for Gershwin's music) largely forgotten today; ironically, his most enduring and respected Broadway work, *Porgy and Bess*, was lukewarmly received upon its premiere in 1935. Gershwin's "American Folk Opera" was inspired by the DuBose Heyward novel *Porgy* (1925) and featured a libretto and lyrics by Ira and the husband-wife team of DuBose and Dorothy Heyward. Theatre critics received the premiere production enthusiastically, but highbrow music critics were derisive, distressed that "lowly" popular music should be incorporated into an opera structure. Black audiences throughout the years have criticized the work for its condescending depiction of stereotyped characters and for Gershwin's inauthentic appropriation of Black musical forms. Nevertheless, Gershwin's music—including such standards as "Summertime," "It Ain't Necessarily So," "Bess, You Is My Woman Now," and "I Got Plenty O' Nuttin"—transcended early criticism to attain a revered niche in the musical world, largely because it successfully amalgamates various musical cultures to evoke something uniquely American and wholly Gershwin.

Aftermath

Gershwin was known as a gregarious man whose huge ego was tempered by a genuinely magnetic personality. He loved his work and approached every assignment with enthusiasm, never suffering from "composer's block." Throughout the first half of 1937, Gershwin began experiencing severe headaches and brief memory blackouts, although medical tests showed him to be in good health. By July, Gershwin exhibited impaired motor skills and drastic weight loss, and he required assistance in walking. He lapsed into a coma on July 9, and a spinal tap revealed the presence of a brain tumour. Gershwin never regained consciousness and died during surgery two days later.

DUKE ELLINGTON

(b. April 29, 1899, Washington, D.C., U.S.—d. May 24, 1974, New York, N.Y.)

American pianist Duke Ellington (born Edward Kennedy Ellington) was one of the most influential jazz composers and bandleaders of the 20th century. One of the originators of big-band jazz, Ellington led his band for more than 50 years, composed thousands of scores, and created one of the most distinctive ensemble sounds in all of Western music.

Ellington grew up in a secure, middle-class family in Washington, D.C. His family encouraged his interests in the fine arts, and he began studying piano at age 7. Inspired by ragtime performers, he began to perform professionally at age 17. On July 2, 1918, a 19-year-old Ellington married Edna Thompson, who had grown up across the street from him. Their son Mercer was born March 11, 1919. (Another child, born the following year, died in infancy.) Ellington first played in New York City in 1923. Later that year he moved there and, in Broadway nightclubs, led a sextet that grew in time into a 10-piece ensemble. The singular blues-based melodies, the harsh, vocalized sounds of his trumpeter, Bubber Miley (who used a plunger ["wa-wa"] mute), and the sonorities of the distinctive trombonist Joe ("Tricky Sam") Nanton (who played muted "growl" sounds) all influenced Ellington's early "jungle style," as seen in such masterpieces as "East St. Louis Toodle-oo" (1926) and "Black and Tan Fantasy" (1927).

Extended residencies at the Cotton Club in Harlem (1927–32, 1937–38) stimulated Ellington to enlarge his band to 14 musicians and to expand his compositional scope. He selected his musicians for their expressive individuality, and several members of his ensemble—including trumpeter Cootie Williams (who replaced Miley), cornetist Rex Stewart, trombonist Lawrence Brown, baritone saxophonist Harry Carney, alto saxophonist Johnny Hodges, and clarinetist Barney Bigard—were themselves important jazz artists. (With these exceptional musicians, who remained with him throughout the 1930s, Ellington made hundreds of recordings, appeared in films and on radio, and toured Europe in 1933 and 1939.

The expertise of this ensemble allowed Ellington to use new harmonies to blend his musicians' individual sounds. He illuminated subtle moods with ingenious combinations of instruments; among the most famous examples is "Mood Indigo" in his 1930 setting for muted trumpet, unmuted trombone, and low-register clarinet. In 1931, Ellington began to create extended works, including such pieces as *Creole Rhapsody, Reminiscing in Tempo*, and *Diminuendo in Blue/Crescendo in Blue*. He composed a series of works to highlight the special talents of his soloists. Williams, for example, demonstrated his versatility in Ellington's miniature concertos *Echoes of Harlem* and *Concerto for Cootie*. Some of Ellington's numbers—notably "Caravan" and "Perdido" by trombonist Juan Tizol—were cowritten or entirely composed by sidemen.

A high point in Ellington's career came in the early 1940s, when he composed several masterworks—including the above-mentioned *Concerto for Cootie*, his fast-tempo showpieces "Cotton Tail" and "Ko-Ko," and the uniquely structured, compressed panoramas "Main

Ellington won 14 Grammy Awards for his music. Three of those he won after he had died.

Stem" and "Harlem Air Shaft"—in which successions of soloists are accompanied by diverse ensemble colours. The variety and ingenuity of these works are extraordinary, as are their unique forms, which range from logically flowing expositions to juxtapositions of line and mood. By then, Billy Strayhorn, composer of what would become the band's theme song, "Take the 'A' Train," had become Ellington's composing-arranging partner.

Not limiting himself to jazz innovation, Ellington also wrote such great popular songs as "Sophisticated Lady," "Rocks in My Bed," and "Satin Doll." In other songs, such as "Don't Get Around Much Any More," "Prelude to a Kiss," and "I Let a Song Go out of My Heart," he made wide interval leaps an Ellington trademark. A number of these hits were introduced by Ivy Anderson, who was the band's female vocalist in the 1930s.

During these years Ellington became intrigued with the possibilities of composing jazz within classical forms. His musical suite *Black, Brown and Beige* (1943), a portrayal of African American history, was the first in a series of suites he composed, usually consisting of pieces linked by subject matter. It was followed by, among others, *Liberian Suite* (1947); *A Drum Is a Woman* (1956), created for a television production; *Such Sweet Thunder* (1957), impressions of William Shakespeare's scenes and characters; a recomposed, reorchestrated version of *Nutcracker Suite* (1960; after Peter Tchaikovsky); *Far East Suite* (1964); and *Togo Brava Suite* (1971). Ellington's symphonic *A Rhapsody of Negro Life* was the basis for the film short *Symphony in Black* (1935). Ellington wrote motion-picture scores for *The Asphalt Jungle* (1950) and *Anatomy of a Murder* (1959) and composed for the ballet and theatre—including, at the height of the civil rights movement, the show *My People* (1964), a celebration of African American life. In his last decade he composed several pieces of sacred music.

Although Ellington's compositional interests and ambitions changed over the decades, his melodic, harmonic, and rhythmic characteristics were for the most part fixed by the late 1930s, when he was a star of the swing era. Ellington's stylistic qualities were shared by Strayhorn, who increasingly participated in composing and orchestrating music for the Ellington band. During 1939–67, Strayhorn collaborated so closely with Ellington that jazz scholars may never determine how much the gifted deputy influenced or even composed works attributed to Ellington.

The Ellington band toured Europe often after World War II; it also played in Asia (1963–64, 1970), West Africa (1966), South America (1968), and Australia (1970) and frequently toured North America. Despite this grueling schedule, some of Ellington's musicians stayed with him for decades; Carney, for example, was a band member for 47 years. For the most part, later replacements fit into roles that had been created by their distinguished predecessors.

Not least of the band's musicians was Ellington himself, a pianist whose style originated in ragtime and the stride piano idiom of James P. Johnson and Willie "The Lion" Smith. He adapted his style for orchestral purposes, accompanying with vivid harmonic colours and, especially in later years, offering swinging solos with angular melodies. An elegant man, Ellington maintained a regal manner as he led the band and charmed audiences with his suave humour. His career spanned more than half a century—most of the documented history of jazz. He continued to lead the band until shortly before his death in 1974.

KURT WEILL

(b. March 2, 1900, Dessau, Ger.—d. April 3, 1950, New York, N.Y., U.S.)

German-born American composer Kurt Julian Weill created a revolutionary kind of opera of sharp social satire in collaboration with the writer Bertolt Brecht.

Weill studied privately with Albert Bing and at the Staatliche Hochschule für Musik in Berlin with Engelbert Humperdinck. He gained some experience as an opera coach and conductor in Dessau and Lüdenscheid (1919–20). Settling in Berlin, he studied (1921–24) under Ferruccio Busoni, beginning as a composer of instrumental works. His early music was expressionistic, experimental, and abstract. His first two operas, *Der Protagonist* (one act, libretto by Georg Kaiser, 1926) and *Royal Palace* (1927), established his position, with Ernst Krenek and Paul Hindemith, as among Germany's most promising young opera composers.

Weill's first collaboration as composer with Bertolt Brecht was on the singspiel (or "songspiel," as he called it) *Mahagonny* (1927), which was a succès de scandale at the Baden-Baden (Germany) Festival in 1927. This work sharply satirizes life in an imaginary America that is also Germany. Weill then wrote the music and Brecht provided the libretto for *Die Dreigroschenoper* (1928; *The Threepenny Opera*), which was a transposition of John Gay's *Beggar's Opera* (1728) with the 18th-century thieves, highwaymen, jailers, and their women turned into typical characters in the Berlin underworld of the 1920s. This work established both the topical opera and the reputations of the composer and librettist. Weill's music for it was in turn harsh, mordant, jazzy, and hauntingly melancholy. *Mahagonny* was elaborated as a full-length opera, *Aufstieg und Fall der Stadt Mahagonny* (composed 1927–29; "Rise and Fall of the City of Mahagonny"), and first presented in Leipzig in 1930. Widely considered Weill's masterpiece, the opera's music showed a skillful synthesis of American popular music, ragtime, and jazz.

Weill's wife, the actress Lotte Lenya (married 1926), sang for the first time in *Mahagonny* and was a great success in it and in *Die Dreigroschenoper*. These works aroused much controversy, as did the students' opera *Der Jasager* (1930; "The Yea-Sayer," with Brecht) and the cantata *Der Lindberghflug* (1928; "Lindbergh's Flight," with Brecht and Hindemith). After the production of the opera *Die Bürgschaft* (1932; "Trust," libretto by Caspar Neher), Weill's political and musical ideas and his Jewish birth made him persona non grata to the Nazis, and he left Berlin for Paris and then for London. His music was banned in Germany until after World War II.

Weill and his wife divorced in 1933 but remarried in 1937 in New York City, where he resumed his career. He wrote music for plays, including Paul Green's *Johnny Johnson* (1936) and Franz Werfel's *Eternal Road* (1937). His operetta *Knickerbocker Holiday* appeared in 1938 with a libretto by Maxwell Anderson, followed by the musical play *Lady in the Dark* (1941; libretto and lyrics by Moss Hart and Ira Gershwin), the musical comedy *One Touch of Venus* (1943; with S. J. Perelman and Ogden Nash), the musical version of Elmer Rice's *Street Scene* (1947), and the musical tragedy *Lost in the Stars* (1949; with Maxwell Anderson). Weill's American folk opera *Down in the Valley* (1948) was much performed. Two of his songs, the "Moritāt" ("Mack the Knife") from *Die Dreigroschenoper* and "September Song" from *Knickerbocker Holiday*, have remained popular. Weill's *Concerto for violin, woodwinds, double bass, and percussion* (1924), *Symphony No. 1* (1921; "Berliner Sinfonie"), and *Symphony No. 2* (1934; "Pariser Symphonie"), works praised for their qualities of invention and compositional skill, were revived after his death.

AARON COPLAND

(b. Nov. 14, 1900, Brooklyn, N.Y., U.S.—d. Dec. 2, 1990, North Tarrytown [now Sleepy Hollow], N.Y.)

American composer Aaron Copland achieved a distinctive musical characterization of American themes in an expressive modern style.

Copland, the son of Russian-Jewish immigrants, was born in New York City and attended public schools there. An older sister taught him to play the piano, and by the time he was 15 he had decided to become a composer. In the summer of 1921, Copland attended the newly founded school for Americans at Fontainebleau, where he came under the influence of Nadia Boulanger, a brilliant teacher who shaped the outlook of an entire generation of American musicians. He decided to stay on in Paris, where he became Boulanger's first American student in composition. After three years in Paris, Copland returned to New York City with an important commission: Nadia Boulanger had asked him to write an organ concerto for her American appearances. Copland composed the piece while working as the pianist of a hotel trio at a summer resort in Pennsylvania. That season the *Symphony for Organ and Orchestra* had its premiere in Carnegie Hall with the New York Symphony.

In his growth as a composer Copland mirrored the important trends of his time. After his return from Paris, he worked with jazz rhythms in *Music for the Theater* (1925) and the *Piano Concerto* (1926). There followed a period during which he was strongly influenced by Igor Stravinsky's neoclassicism, turning toward an abstract style he described as "more spare in sonority, more lean in texture." This outlook prevailed in the *Piano Variations* (1930), *Short Symphony* (1933), and *Statements for Orchestra* (1933–35). After this last work, there occurred a change of direction that was to

American composer Aaron Copland created a large volume of work building on different styles throughout the 20th century.

usher in the most productive phase of Copland's career. He realized that a new public for modern music was being created by the new media of radio, phonograph, and film scores: "It made no sense to ignore them and to continue writing as if they did not exist. I felt that it was worth the effort to see if I couldn't say what I had to say in the simplest possible terms." Copland therefore was led to what became a most significant development after the 1930s: the attempt to simplify the new music in order that it would have meaning for a large public.

The decade that followed saw the production of the scores that spread Copland's fame throughout the world. Most important of these were the three ballets based on American folk material: *Billy the Kid* (1938), *Rodeo* (1942), and *Appalachian Spring* (1944; commissioned by dancer Martha Graham). To this group belonged also *El salón México* (1936), an orchestral piece based on Mexican melodies and rhythms; two works for high-school students—the "play opera" *The Second Hurricane* (1937) and *An Outdoor Overture* (1938); and a series of film scores, of which the best known are *Of Mice and Men* (1939), *Our Town* (1940), *The Red Pony* (1948), and *The Heiress* (1948). Typical too of the Copland style are two major works that were written in time of war—*Lincoln Portrait* (1942), for speaker and chorus, on a text drawn from Lincoln's speeches, and *Letter from Home* (1944), as well as the melodious *Third Symphony* (1946).

In his later years Copland refined his treatment of Americana: "I no longer feel the need of seeking out conscious Americanism. Because we live here and work here, we can be certain that when our music is mature it will also be American in quality." His later works include an opera, *The Tender Land* (1954); *Twelve Poems of Emily Dickinson* (1950), for voice and piano; and the delightful *Nonet* (1960). During these years Copland also produced a number of works in which he showed himself increasingly receptive to the serial techniques of the so-called 12-tone school of composer Arnold Schoenberg. Notable among such works are the stark and dissonant *Piano Fantasy* (1957); *Connotations* (1962), which was commissioned for the opening of Lincoln Center for the Performing Arts in New York City; and *Inscape* (1967). The 12-tone works were not generally well received; after 1970 Copland virtually stopped composing, though he continued to lecture and to conduct through the mid-1980s.

For the better part of four decades, as composer (of operas, ballets, orchestral music, band music, chamber music, choral music, and film scores), teacher, writer of books and articles on music, organizer of musical events, and a much sought-after conductor, Copland expressed "the deepest reactions of the American consciousness to the American scene." He received more than 30 honorary degrees and many additional awards. He also wrote a number of books on music.

A private man not given to making public statements about his personal life, Copland nonetheless made no efforts to hide his homosexuality, traveling openly with younger lovers. And though blacklisted during the McCarthy era, the government-led censure had no lasting effect on Copland's work and career.

LOUIS ARMSTRONG

(b. Aug. 4, 1901, New Orleans, La., U.S.—d. July 6, 1971, New York, N.Y.)

Louis Armstrong, or Satchmo (a truncation of "Satchel Mouth"), was the leading trumpeter and one of the most influential artists in jazz history.

Armstrong grew up in dire poverty in New Orleans, La., when jazz was very young. As a child he worked at odd jobs and sang in a boys' quartet. In 1913, he was sent to the Colored Waifs Home as a juvenile delinquent. There he learned to play cornet in the home's band, and playing music quickly became a passion. Armstrong developed rapidly: he played in marching and jazz bands, becoming skillful enough to replace New Orleans jazz cornetist King Oliver in the important Kid Ory band in about 1918, and in the early 1920s he played in Mississippi riverboat dance bands.

Fame beckoned in 1922 when Oliver, then leading a band in Chicago, sent for Armstrong to play second cornet. Oliver's Creole Jazz Band was the apex of the early, contrapuntal New Orleans ensemble style, and it included musicians such as the brothers Johnny and Baby Dodds and pianist Lil Hardin, who married Armstrong in 1924. The young Armstrong became popular through his ingenious ensemble lead and second cornet lines, his cornet duet passages (called "breaks") with Oliver, and his solos. He recorded his first solos as a member of the Oliver band in such pieces as "Chimes Blues" and "Tears."

Encouraged by his wife, Armstrong quit Oliver's band to seek further fame. He played for a year in New York City in Fletcher Henderson's band and on many recordings with others before returning to Chicago and playing in large orchestras. There he created his most important early works, the Armstrong Hot Five and Hot Seven recordings of 1925–28, on which he emerged as the first great jazz soloist. By then the New Orleans ensemble style, which allowed few solo opportunities, could no longer contain his explosive creativity. He retained vestiges of the style in such masterpieces as "Hotter Than That," "Struttin' with Some Barbecue," "Wild Man Blues," and "Potato Head Blues" but largely abandoned it while accompanied by pianist Earl Hines ("West End Blues" and "Weather Bird"). By that time Armstrong was playing trumpet, and his technique was superior to that of all competitors. Altogether, his immensely compelling swing, his brilliant technique, his sophisticated, daring sense of harmony, his ever-mobile, expressive attack, timbre, and inflections, his gift for creating vital melodies; his dramatic, often complex sense of solo design, and his outsized musical energy and genius made these recordings major innovations in jazz.

Armstrong was a famous musician by 1929, when he moved from Chicago to New York City and performed in the theatre review *Hot Chocolates*. He toured America and Europe as a trumpet soloist accompanied by big bands; for several years beginning in 1935, Luis Russell's big band served as the Louis Armstrong band. During this time he abandoned much of the material of his earlier years for popular songs by such composers as Hoagy Carmichael, Irving Berlin, and Duke Ellington. With his new repertoire came a new, simplified style: he created melodic paraphrases and variations as well as chord-change-based improvisations on these songs. His trumpet range continued to expand, as demonstrated in the high-note showpieces in his repertoire. His beautiful tone and bravura solos with brilliant high-note climaxes led to such masterworks as "That's My Home," "Body and Soul," and "Star Dust." One of the inventors of scat singing, he began to sing lyrics on most of his recordings, varying melodies or decorating with scat phrases in a gravel voice that was immediately identifiable. Although he sang such humorous songs as "Hobo, You Can't Ride This Train," he also sang many standard songs, often with an intensity and creativity that equaled those of his trumpet playing.

Louis and Lil Armstrong separated in 1931. From 1935 to the end of his life, Armstrong's career was managed by Joe Glaser, who hired Armstrong's bands and guided his film career (beginning with *Pennies from Heaven*, 1936) and radio appearances. Armstrong was the dominant influence on the swing era, when most trumpeters attempted to emulate his inclination to dramatic structure, melody, or technical

Although Armstrong performed during the mid-twentieth century, many of his songs are still wildly popular today.

virtuosity. Trombonists, too, appropriated Armstrong's phrasing, and saxophonists as different as Coleman Hawkins and Bud Freeman modeled their styles on different aspects of Armstrong's. Above all else, his swing-style trumpet playing influenced virtually all jazz horn players who followed him, and the swing of his vocal style was an important influence on singers from Billie Holiday to Bing Crosby.

In most of Armstrong's movie, radio, and television appearances, he was featured as a good-humoured entertainer. He played a rare dramatic role in the film *New Orleans* (1947), in which he also performed in a Dixieland band. This prompted the formation of Louis Armstrong's All-Stars, a Dixieland band that at first included such other jazz greats as Hines and trombonist Jack Teagarden. For most of the rest of Armstrong's life, he toured the world with changing All-Stars sextets. It was the period of his greatest popularity; he produced hit recordings such as "Mack the Knife" and "Hello, Dolly!" and outstanding albums such as his tributes to W.C. Handy and Fats Waller. In his last years ill health curtailed his trumpet playing, but he continued as a singer. His last film appearance was in *Hello, Dolly!* (1969), but his most memorable film role may well be as narrator of and bandleader in the 1956 hit musical *High Society*, also starring Frank Sinatra, Bing Crosby, and Grace Kelly.

More than a great trumpeter, Armstrong was a bandleader, singer, soloist, film star, and comedian. One of his most remarkable feats was his frequent conquest of the popular market. He nonetheless made his greatest impact on the evolution of jazz itself, which at the start of his career was popularly considered to be little more than a novelty. With his great sensitivity, technique, and capacity to express emotion, Armstrong not only ensured the survival of jazz but led in its development into a fine art.

UMM KULTHŪM

(b. May 4, 1904?, Tummāy al-Zahāyrah, Egypt—d. Feb. 3, 1975, Cairo)

Egyptian singer Umm Kulthūm mesmerized Arab audiences from the Persian Gulf to Morocco for half a century. She was one of the most famous Arab singers and public personalities in the 20th century.

Umm Kulthūm's father was a village imam who sang traditional religious songs at weddings and holidays to make ends meet. She learned to sing from him, and, when he noticed the strength of her voice, he began taking her with him, dressed as a boy to avoid the opprobrium of displaying a young daughter onstage. Egyptian society during Umm Kulthūm's youth held singing—even of the religious variety—to be a disreputable occupation, especially for a female. Umm Kulthūm made a name for herself singing in the towns and villages of the Egyptian delta (an area throughout which she retained a great following). By the time she was a teenager, she had become the family star.

Sometime about 1923 the family moved to Cairo, a major centre of the lucrative world of entertainment and emerging mass media production in the Middle East. There they were perceived as old-fashioned and countrified. To improve her image and acquire sophistication, Umm Kulthūm studied music and poetry from accomplished performers and literati and copied the manners of the ladies of wealthy homes in which she was invited to sing. She soon made a name in the homes and salons of the wealthy as well as in public venues such as theatres and cabarets. By the mid-1920s she had made her first recordings and had achieved a more polished and sophisticated musical and personal style. By the end of the 1920s, she had become a sought-after performer and was one of the best-paid musicians in Cairo. Her extremely successful career in commercial recording eventually extended to radio, film, and television. In 1936 she made her first motion picture, *Wedad*, in which she played the title role. It was the first of six motion pictures in which she was to act.

Beginning in 1937, she regularly gave a performance on the first Thursday (which in most Islamic countries is the last day of the workweek) of every month. By this time she had moved from singing religious songs to performing popular tunes—often in the colloquial dialect and accompanied by a small traditional orchestra—and she became known for her emotive, passionate renditions of arrangements by the best composers, poets, and songwriters of the day. These included the poets Aḥmad Shawqī and Bayrām al-Tūnisī (who wrote many of the singer's colloquial Egyptian songs) and, later, the noted composer Muḥammad 'Abd al-Wahhāb, with whom she collaborated on 10 songs. The first of these tunes, "Inta 'Umrī" ("You Are My Life"), remains a modern classic. Her strong and nuanced voice and her ability to fashion multiple iterations of single lines of text drew audiences into the emotion and meaning of the poetic lyrics and extended for hours what often had been written as relatively short compositions.

Known sometimes as Kawkab al-Sharq ("Star of the East"), Umm Kulthūm had an immense repertoire, which included religious, sentimental, and nationalistic songs. In the midst of the turmoil created by two world wars, the Great Depression of the 1930s, and the 1952 Egyptian revolution, she cultivated a public persona as a patriotic Egyptian and a devout Muslim. She sang songs in support of Egyptian independence ("Nashīd al-Jāmi'ah" ["The University Anthem"], "Sa'alu Qalbī" ["Ask My Heart"]) and in the 1950s sang many songs in support of Egyptian leader Gamal Abdel Nasser, with whom she developed a close friendship. One of her songs associated with Nasser—"Wallāhi Zamān, Yā

Silāḥī" ("It's Been a Long Time, O Weapon of Mine")—was adopted as the Egyptian national anthem from 1960 to 1979. She served as president of the Musician's Union for seven years and held positions on numerous government commissions on the arts. Her popularity was further enhanced by her generous donations to Arab causes. After Egypt's defeat in the Six-Day War of June 1967, she toured Egypt and the broader Arab world, donating the proceeds of her concerts to the Egyptian government.

Health problems plagued the singer most of her life. During the late 1940s and early '50s, she worked only on a limited basis, and on a number of occasions throughout her life she traveled to Europe and the United States for treatment of a variety of ailments. Most obviously, problems with her eyes (purportedly from years spent in front of stage lights) forced her to wear heavy sunglasses, which became a hallmark during her later life. Such was her popularity that news of her death provoked a spontaneous outpouring of hysterical grief, and millions of admirers lined the streets for her funeral procession. She remained one of the Arab world's best-selling singers even decades after her death. In 2001, the Egyptian government established the Kawkab al-Sharq Museum in Cairo to celebrate the singer's life and accomplishments.

Glossary

amalgam: A fusion of different elements.

assiduity: Great and persistent attention and diligence.

avant-garde: Experimental or progressive.

blacklisting: Creating a list of people to be shunned, especially in reference to suspected Communist supporters in 1950s American culture.

bravura: A style of music that is highly difficult and intended to show off the skill of the performer.

cantata: A poem set to music as a lyric drama, but not enacted.

chromatic: Notes that are half-steps or semitones apart; on a piano, the difference in sound between a white key and the closest black key.

contrapuntal: Characterized by two or more independent melodies sounded together.

diatonic: A scale of the type represented by the white keys on a piano.

dissonance: Lack of a consonant (agreeable) sound between two or more tones.

opprobrium: Disgrace resulting from shameful conduct.

oratorio: A musical composition for voices and orchestra that tells a sacred story without costumes, scenery, or dramatic action.

proletarian: A member of the working class.

recapitulation: The final section of a musical composition that repeats the earlier themes.

singspiel: A type of German comic opera that mixes light songs with spoken passages.

For More Information

BOOKS

Crawford, Richard. *Summertime: George Gershwin's Life in Music.* New York, NY: W. W. Norton & Company, 2019.

Musegades, Paula. *Aaron Copland's Hollywood Film Scores.* Rochester, NY: University of Rochester Press, 2020.

Palazzetti, Nicolò. *Béla Bartók in Italy: The Politics of Myth-Making.* Woodbridge, England: The Boydell Press, 2021.

Riccardi, Ricky. *Heart Full of Rhythm: The Big Band Years of Louis Armstrong.* New York, NY: Oxford University Press, 2020.

WEBSITES

Carter Family

www.countrymusichalloffame.org/hall-of-fame/carter-family

The Country Music Hall of Fame website has more background and song clips from the Carter Family.

Charles Ives Society

www.charlesives.org/

Learn more about composer Charles Ives at the website for the Charles Ives Society, a nonprofit group that encourages the performance of his music.

Umm Kulthūm's Museum

www.cairo.gov.eg/en/Culture/Pages/Cairo-Museums-details.aspx?ID=2

Learn more about singer Umm Kulthūm at the Egyptian government's website for a museum dedicated to her.

Index